SPORTS CAR
RACING

BY MAE RESPICIO

CAPSTONE PRESS
a capstone imprint

Published by Spark, an imprint of Capstone
1710 Roe Crest Drive, North Mankato, Minnesota 56003
capstonepub.com

Library of Congress Cataloging-in-Publication Data
Names: Respicio, Mae, author.
Title: Sports car racing / by Mae Respicio.
Description: North Mankato, Minnesota : Capstone Press, [2025] | Series: Powerful sports cars | Includes bibliographical references and index. | Audience: Ages 9-11 | Audience: Grades 4-6 | Summary: "VEEERRM! Did you see those sleek cars streaking by? They're competing in one of the world's most popular events—sports car racing! From the 12 Hours of Sebring to the 24 Hours of Daytona, drivers in the world's fastest sports cars race to see who will come out on top. Take a trip to the track and discover which cars have found success in the world of sports car racing"— Provided by publisher.
Identifiers: LCCN 2024010312 (print) | LCCN 2024010313 (ebook) | ISBN 9781669079101 (hardcover) | ISBN 9781669079057 (paperback) | ISBN 9781669079064 (pdf) | ISBN 9781669079088 (kindle edition) | ISBN 9781669079071 (epub)
Subjects: LCSH: Automobile racing—Juvenile literature. | Sports cars—Juvenile literature.
Classification: LCC GV1029.13 .R47 2025 (print) | LCC GV1029.13 (ebook) | DDC 796.72—dc23/eng/20240318
LC record available at https://lccn.loc.gov/2024010312
LC ebook record available at https://lccn.loc.gov/2024010313

Editorial Credits
Editor: Carrie Sheely; Designer: Elyse White; Media Researcher: Svetlana Zhurkin; Production Specialist: Tori Abraham

Image Credits
Getty Images: AFP/Fred Tanneau, 23, AFP/Jean-Francois Monier, 11, 28, Brian Cleary, 9, 10, 25, 29, Clive Rose, 1, Eurasia Sport Images/Laurent Cartalade, 17, Icon Sportswire/David Rosenblum, 27, ISC Images & Archives, 13, James Moy Photography, 16, 21; Newscom: Heritage Images/National Motor Museum, 6; Shutterstock: Alexandria Bates, 8, Brendt A. Petersen, cover (top right), Dan74, 5, 14, Frolphy, 19, Jean Pierre Kathoefer, 26, Jens Mommens, 22, Oskar Schuler, 7, ParabolStudio, cover (top left and bottom), Steve Lagreca, 15, WinWin artlab (design element), cover and throughout, YES Market Media, 18, 20

Printed and bound in the USA. 5853

CONTENTS

Words in **bold** are in the glossary.

RACING ROOTS

A sleek sports car speeds around the track. The driver steps on the gas pedal. *Zoom!* The car gets faster. It's at top speed! The car zips past another car. It roars through twists and turns. Will it win the race?

How did sports car racing start? It began with a need for speed.

The history of car racing dates back to the 1880s. People began racing soon after **gasoline**-powered engines were invented. The first organized race was in 1894 in France. Today, car racing is loved around the world.

A car in the 1894 race

There are many types of car races. Just like cars on the streets, racing sports cars have **fenders** around the wheels. The race cars are designed for speed. They can go both fast and far.

Some races are professional. The drivers compete for a living. Other races are for **amateurs**. These drivers compete for fun.

Professional drivers Pipo Derani, Mike Conway, and Tristan Nunez (left to right) celebrate a race win.

What are two important parts of sports car racing? Speed and **stamina**. The races test the toughness of a car. Many races go for a certain length of time. Some go for 24 hours. Since the races are so long, the cars are built to last.

FACT

In 2010, Audi team drivers broke a record for going the farthest distance at the 24 Hours of Le Mans. They went 3,362 miles (5,410 kilometers).

SPEED MACHINES

Ferraris are some of the most popular kinds of race cars. One **legendary** model is the Ferrari 250 GTO. It competed in many races during the 1960s. Only 36 of them exist today.

A Ferrari 250 GTO leading a 1963 race

Lamborghini Huracán GT3 in a race

Lamborghinis are speedy sports cars too. One of the most famous models is the Lamborghini Huracán GT3. They compete in races around the world. Do they often win? Yes!

Chevrolet Corvettes have a long racing history. In 2023, the Corvette team drivers won the 24 Hours of Le Mans in a Corvette C8.R. It was the ninth time the team has won the famous race.

FACT

The Corvette Mako Shark's sleek design led to racing versions of the Corvette. People thought the car's body design made it look like a shark.

TOP-NOTCH TEAMS

Racetracks have different shapes. A sports car track is tricky. It has sharp turns and uneven surfaces. This makes racing hard. Each race has its own set of rules.

But before a car can race, what does it need? Daring drivers!

Professional race car drivers are part of skilled teams. Besides drivers, a team has managers, **mechanics**, and **engineers**. They work together to get the cars ready to race. Why? They want to win!

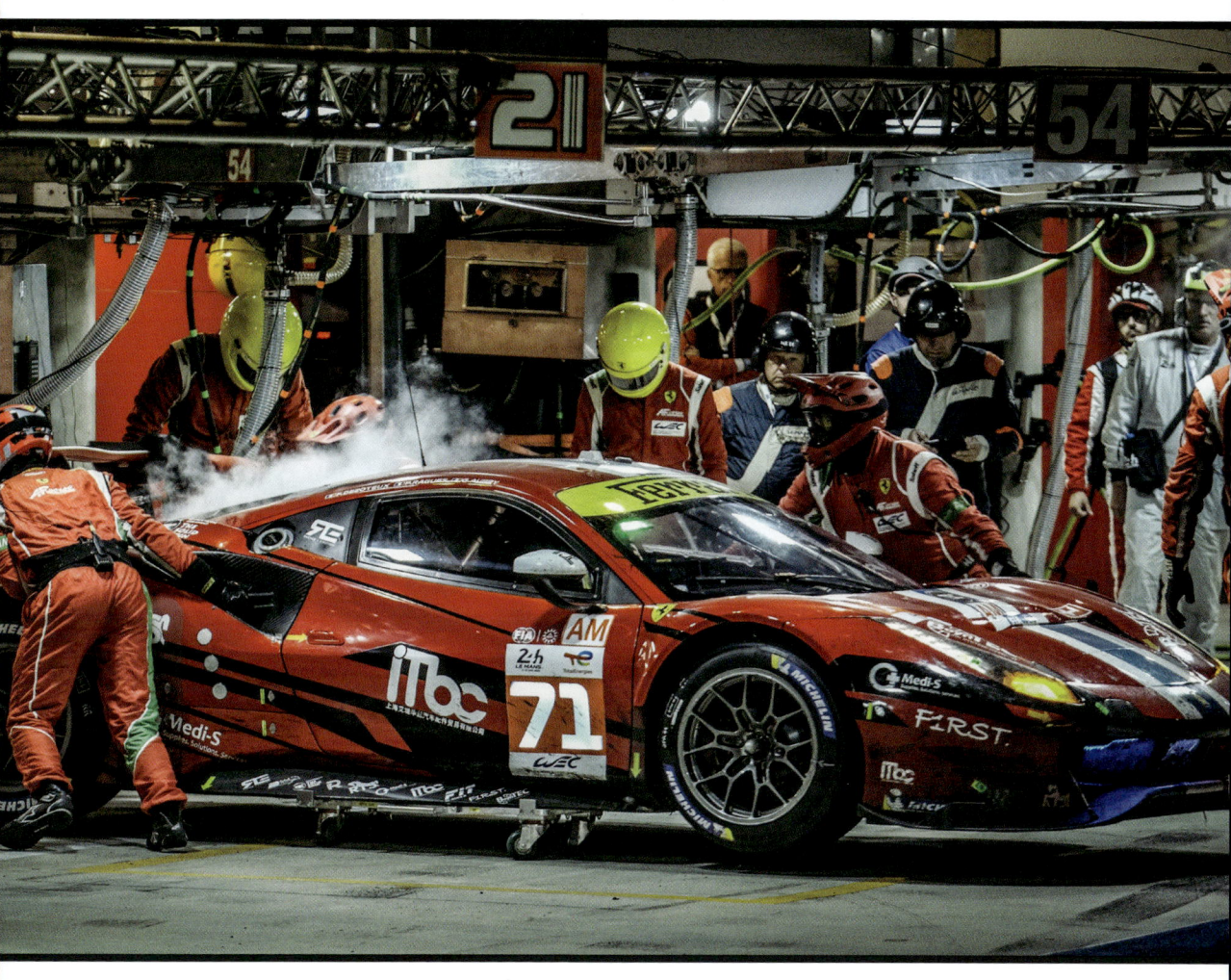

During races, the cars make **pit stops** for fuel and to change the tires. Pit stops are important to make sure a car races at its best. They happen very fast. In a 24-hour race, a car may make about 27 stops.

FACT

Duct tape is sometimes used to quickly repair damaged car parts during a race.

FAST TRACKS

The 24 Hours of Le Mans is one of the oldest sports car races. It takes place in Le Mans, France. This race is **demanding**. Drivers often push the cars to speeds near 200 miles (322 km) per hour. They need to brake quickly for turns. Drivers have to stay focused.

Ferrari drivers celebrate their win at the 2023 24 Hours of Le Mans.

The winner is the team that covers the most distance. Porsche, Audi, and Ferrari have the most wins at this race.

Another famous race is the 12 Hours of Sebring. It is held in Sebring, Florida. It lasts for 12 hours straight.

The track is bumpy with different surfaces. The race often happens in hot, **humid** weather. This makes it a challenge for drivers.

Weather conditions can be unpredictable in Florida when the 24 Hours of Daytona is held. Racers may face rain and fog.

The 24 Hours of Daytona is held in Daytona Beach, Florida. The track has **hairpin turns**. It can be hard to pass other cars. One mistake can cause a crash. Winning is a big deal! Winning drivers receive a Rolex watch.

On race day, engines roar. Fans cheer. Cars zoom down the track. The checkered flag goes down. The race is finished! The winning team celebrates by driving in victory lane. What a thrill!

GLOSSARY

amateur (AM-uh-chur)—an athlete who is not paid for participating in a sport

demanding (di-MAN-ding)—requiring much time, effort, or attention

engineer (en-juh-NEER)—a person trained to use science and math to design and build machines

fender (FEN-duhr)—a cover over a car's wheel

gasoline (GA-suh-leen)—a liquid fuel made from oil

hairpin turn (HAYR-pin TURN)—a sharp U-shaped turn on a road or racetrack

humid (HYOO-mid)—damp or moist

legendary (LEJ-uhnd-air-ee)—known for accomplishing great things

mechanic (muh-KAN-ik)—someone who fixes vehicles or machinery

pit stop (PIT STOP)—a break drivers take from the race so the pit crew can add fuel, change tires, and make repairs to a car

stamina (STAM-uh-nuh)—the energy and strength to keep doing something for a long time

READ MORE

Flynn, Brendan. *Car Racing Records Smashed!* North Mankato, MN: Capstone, 2024.

Goldsworthy, Steve. *The Tech Behind Race Cars.* North Mankato, MN: Capstone, 2020.

Rendle, Steve. *Sports Cars*. New York: PowerKids Press, 2022.

INTERNET SITES

Ferrari: Hypercar
ferrari.com/en-US/hypercar

International Motor Sports Association (IMSA)
imsa.com

Porsche: Formula E, GT, Esports, and Customer Racing at its Best
porsche.com/usa/motorsportandevents
/motorsport

INDEX

ABOUT THE AUTHOR

Mae Respicio is a nonfiction writer and middle grade author. Her novel, *The House That Lou Built*, won an Asian Pacific American Libraries Association Honor Award and was an NPR Best Book. Mae has fun childhood memories of cruising around California with her dad in his 1968 classic Ford Mustang.